Union Public Library
1980 Morris Avenue
Union, N.J. 07083

P9-CMT-474

Grand Canyon

Union Public Library
1980 Morris Avenue
Union, N.J. 07083

By Lisa Trumbauer

Consultant
Nanci R. Vargus, Ed.D.
Assistant Professor of Literacy
University of Indianapolis, Indianapolis, Indiana

Children's Press®
A Division of Scholastic Inc.
New York Toronto London Auckland Sydney
Mexico City New Delhi Hong Kong
Danbury, Connecticut

Designer: Herman Adler Design
Photo Researcher: Caroline Anderson
The photo on the cover shows the Grand Canyon.

Library of Congress Cataloging-in-Publication Data

Trumbauer, Lisa, 1963-
  Grand Canyon / By Lisa Trumbauer.
      p. cm. — (Rookie read-about geography)
  Includes index.
  ISBN 0-516-22747-5 (lib.bdg.)   0-516-25931-8 (pbk.)
  1. Grand Canyon (Ariz.)—Juvenile literature. I. Title. II. Series.
  F788.T79 2005
  917.91'32—dc22
                                    2004015574

©2005 by Scholastic Inc.
All rights reserved. Published simultaneously in Canada.
Printed in the United States of America.

CHILDREN'S PRESS, and ROOKIE READ-ABOUT®,
and associated logos are trademarks and or registered trademarks
of Scholastic Library Publishing. SCHOLASTIC and associated logos
are trademarks and or registered trademarks of Scholastic Inc.

1 2 3 4 5 6 7 8 9 10 R 14 13 12 11 10 09 08 07 06 05

The Grand Canyon is one of the biggest canyons in the world.

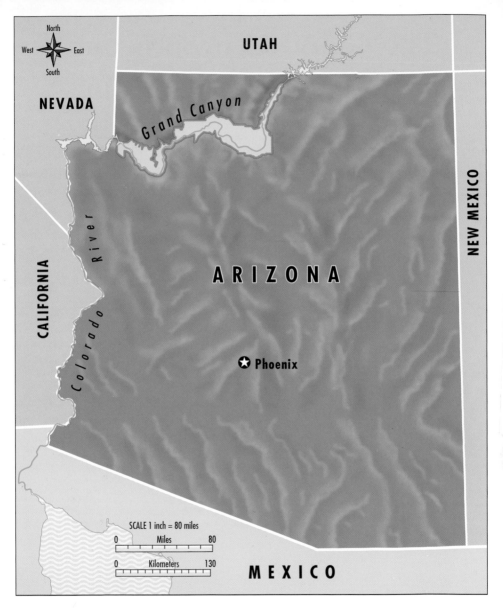

North
West East
South

UTAH

NEVADA

Grand Canyon

NEW MEXICO

CALIFORNIA

Colorado River

ARIZONA

⭐ Phoenix

SCALE 1 inch = 80 miles

0   Miles   80

0   Kilometers   130

MEXICO

What is a canyon? A canyon is a long, deep valley.

Can you find the Grand Canyon on this map?

The Grand Canyon is in Arizona.

The Grand Canyon is 277 miles long.

It is over 1 mile deep in some places. It is 18 miles across at its widest point!

The Colorado River flows through the Grand Canyon.

The moving water carved out the canyon over millions of years.

Colorado River

10

The canyon walls have many layers of rock and soil.

The layers give the canyon its striped colors. The colors come from the minerals in the rock.

Native Americans have lived along the canyon for about 4,000 years.

Today, the Havasupai live inside the canyon. They live in the village of Supai.

To get to Supai, you have to hike there. You can get there by helicopter, too.

Most of the Grand Canyon is a national park.

The land in a national park is protected.

Many people like to hike in
Grand Canyon National Park.

Some people hike along the canyon's north and south rims. The rims are the edges of the canyon.

Some people ride mules
into the canyon.

Some people look at the
canyon from the air!

Some people go rafting. They raft on the Colorado River at the bottom of the canyon.

These people camp inside
the canyon.

The weather at the Grand Canyon is mostly dry.

It doesn't rain much. Some parts of the Grand Canyon get only 6 inches of rain a year.

Ponderosa pine grow outside the canyon.

Cactuses and shrubs grow inside the canyon.

Mule deer live outside
the canyon.

Desert bighorn sheep
climb inside the canyon.

The Grand Canyon is an amazing place to visit.

What do you want to see at the Grand Canyon?

Words You Know

Arizona

cactus

desert bighorn sheep

Grand Canyon

30

mule

mule deer

ponderosa pine

rafting

31

Index

animals, 26–27

Arizona, 5

camping, 21

canyons, 3, 5

color, 11

Colorado River, 8, 20

desert bighorn sheep, 27

Havasupai Indians, 12

hiking, 16-17

layers, 11

length, 6

minerals, 11

mule deer, 26

mule rides, 18

national parks, 15

Native Americans, 12

plants, 24–25

rafting, 20

rain, 23

rims, 17

rocks, 11

Supai (village), 12

valleys, 5

visitors, 16–21

walls, 11

weather, 23

About the Author

Lisa Trumbauer is the author of nearly 200 books for kids. She and her husband Dave love to travel, following their favorite baseball team, the Baltimore Orioles, around the United States. During one ten-day trip, they squeezed in eight ballgames at 6 different ballparks. They even managed to see the Grand Canyon.

Photo Credits

Photographs © 2005: Bob Clemenz Photography/Bob & Suzanne Clemenz: cover, 3, 22, 30 bottom right; Corbis Images: 14 (L. Clarke), 25, 30 top (Kevin Fleming), 21 (Craig Lovell), 13 (Mark Peterson), 29 (Ron Watts); Dave G. Houser/HouserStock, Inc./Ellen Barone: 19, 20, 31 bottom right; Dembinsky Photo Assoc./Scott T. Smith: 24, 31 bottom left; Peter Arnold Inc.: 26, 31 top right (David J. Cross), 16 (Oldrich Karasek); Photo Researchers, NY: 7, 9 (Mark Newman), 18, 31 top left (N.R. Rowan), 10 (Jim Steinberg); The Image Bank/Getty Images/Joseph Van Os: 27, 30 bottom left.

Maps by Bob Italiano